TO

My sweethearts

FROM

~~[scribbled out]~~

Victoria
B. Fou ♥

©CARLTON CARDS, CLEVELAND, OH MADE IN U.S.A.

ISBN 1-56218-027-4

I Said a Prayer for You Today

I said
a prayer
for you today,
the way
I often do...

I asked the Lord
to fill your days
with warmth
and blessings, too.

I told Him
you were dear to me
and prayed
He'd be your guide...

...to help you choose
what's best for you
in all that you decide.

I asked the Lord
   to lend His hand
to everything
     you start...

...and, with His love,
help you fulfill
the dreams
within your heart.

I asked Him
to stay close to you,
to hear you
    when you call...

...and give to you
life's sweetest gifts,
for you deserve
them all!

You're
in my prayers
and
in my thoughts...

...more often
than you know.

I ♥ u

I ♥ you